DRAWN

TO

LEADERSHIP

ISBN 979-8-218-11784-9 (Paperback)
Drawn to Leadership
Copyright © 2022 Tehron Jaqui Bush

DRAWN

TO

LEADERSHIP

Tehron Jaqui Bush

CONTENTS

Chapter 1:   The Reason Why 1
Chapter 2:   To Notice and For Improvement 5
Chapter 3:   A New Call for Response 18
Chapter 4:   My Leadership Posture 20
Chapter 5:   Charity & Christian Leadership 22
Chapter 6:   Study the Rules 25
Chapter 7:   Empower the Public, Not Policy 30
Chapter 8:   The Best Model 33
Chapter 9:   Embrace and Replenish Resources 35
Chapter 10: Contemporary Leadership 40
Chapter 11: Drawn to Leadership 46

Works Cited 55
References 57

Special Thank You

Marissa Bush, Deloris Bush, Cayden Price Worley, Delaney Kathryn Worley-Bush, Ronald Bush, Sonja Woodlief-Stonework, Cheryl Worley, James Worley, Jennifer Vandermeer-Worley, Breelyn Worley, Cameron Worley, Zachary Worley, Julia Worley, Kayla Worley, Jyron Caywood, Stephen Dillard, Charles Bush, Torra Robinson, Scott Bush, Sidney Bush, Torry Robinson, Tonya Kirkland, Donald Kirkland, Keenan Kirkland, Caleb Kirkland, Carolyn Hunt, Frank Hunt, Damon Hunt, Kathleen Hunt, Phyllis Worley, Royal Chavious, MacKenzie Chavious, Kenneth Evans Jr., Robin Brown, Tishawnda McNair, Dexter McNair, Darrick Williams, Malik Williams, Leslie Brown, Maurice Brown, James Evans, James Evans Jr., Rosemary Brown, Willie Brown, Steffon Brown, Norma Rhodes, Mark Mosely, Dorothy Mosely, Kristoph Williams, Nicholas Spangler, Judy Spangler, Ian Spangler, Eric Spangler, Corrine Spangler, Erin Reisman, Michael Reisman, Chelsea Reisman, Shea Reisman, Zoe Reisman, Albert Chaney, Xavier Hunt, Sebastien Hunt, Emilien Hunt, Alexiane Hunt, Mozelle Banks, Shannon Snowden, Christian Snowden, Paulette Snowden, Virginia "Deeney" Lee, John "John-John" Smith, Paul Martin, Janie Mae Wynn, Irvin Brown, J.T. Powell, John Powell, Jake Powell, Nancy Powell, Ebonnie Simmons, James Simmons & Sandra Simmons.

1

The Reason Why

L eadership can get defined as delivering a group or organization to an objective, goal, or means of an end. Today's cur- rent and popular traditionalleadershipstyleisthetop-down hierarchal method. Strong leaders are compassionate, good listeners, community-driven, and pioneering. Leadership must express the needs, ideas, and goals of the group or organization's majority to succeed. Leadership today encompasses a diverse population or heterogeneous mixture of races, cultures, and ethnicities. The government and the private business sectors must teach a good leadership model. A good leadership model examines successful attributes from strong leaders in other regions and incorporates practices into its leadership model. There is a need for a global leadership model due to changes in a borderless economy. Strong leadership models and leaders need implementation in groups and organizations where corruption and organizational structure have collapsed.

The purpose of leadership is to deliver objectives, goals, or results for a group or organization. Leadership intends to make ideas into objectives. Leaders use education and experience to guide and direct group and organization members toward insightful objectives. Leadership aims to teach group and organization memberstoteach and train non-leaders if a current leader leaves the group or organization. For example, a current leader may leave a group or organization for retirement. A leader must teach the group or orga- nization a model of sustainability. A new leader must emerge when a leader leaves to carry on a group or organization function. A leader must develop the roles, skills, characters, and attributes of the group members for the best approach to the group or organizational problem-solving. The traditional leadership model ignores the ideas of the group or organization and instead emphasizes individualism, meritocracy, free market, and competition. The need for character-based leadership can get found in government organizations as well as business organizations. Leadership aims to liber- ate groups and organizations from reoccurring problems based upon experience to achieve a targeted result. Strong leadership is restorative and continuous and aims to provide order for a group or organization. A growing mixed population within the United States calls for a new inclusive leadership model in government and business organizations.

Many qualities are admirable in a leader. A thoughtful leader can sacrifice personal gain and practice self-constraint to empower the group or organization. A good leader becomes very educated about the problems the group or organization faces to deliver expected results. A leader must have a vision. A pioneer by "heart," a leader sees a vision that no group member shares. The leader sets goals based on visionary development for the group or organization. A strong leader is resourceful. The leader knows the location of essential materials or information for task completion in the group or organization. An intelligent leader can explain a process or procedure needed for completion so that the entire group or organization can function cohesively. Leaders must reeducate new, emerging leaders to achieve leadership positions within a group or organization. Leaders must train new members to learn, reproach, and reprocess to strengthen and sustain a group or organization, and a trustworthy leader does not misrepresent the group or organization. Instead, the leader is a facilitator and stimulates collective group action. A focused leader has great organizational skills, and decision-making based on reason, rationality, and analytics.

An effective leader knows when to redirect the group or orga- nization when off task or misguided. A good leader has experience in their field of study, and this leader has many examples to draw ideas and experiences to minimize risk and exposure to loss and disfranchisement.

As a leader, my peers may say I embody certain leadership traits. I encompass active listening skills within my groups and organiza- tions. I like to listen to all sides of conflict before I offer any solution or open dialogue. As a leader, I teach my groups and my organization's comprehensive approach to problem-solving. I do this so every- one understands the problem completely. A well-explained problem allows for a well-thought-out answer. I believe I am resourceful. I try to find contemporary, cost-effective, and qualitative sources, especially with my Christian clothing brand, Stizo Collection. I have a heterogeneous approach to problem-solving. As a leader, I am honest. I will not tell my group or organization informa- tion or ideas that do not belong to us. Good or bad news, a "reality check" once in a while sparks group or organization productivity.

As an emerging leader, I wish to develop more important leadership qualities in character for decision-making, community-based involvement, re-teaching leadership, and leadership consistency. A moral leader develops a stronger character. A moral leader acts in faith for just character. Despite race, religion, ethnic, or cultural differences, a leader must learn to be sensitive to all human life for the greater good.

A strong leader needs to make decisions based on the total picture, not from materialistic or capitalistic wants but from the needs of the less heard and marginalized people in society. Empower global reform and global economic expansion, then offer the luxuries of western culture to the world.

An inclusive leader is a community leader. The United States is a heterogeneous community. Therefore, the United States needs heterogeneous "democratic republic community" leaders to encompass future collective global leadership models.

The best leadership models need replenishment, "the best of the best." Education removes the source of ignorance. Re-teaching superior leadership bestows superior leaders.

Not only do leaders need these qualities, but leaders need these qualities consistently. Good leadership needs continuity and sparsity. A leader here, or a good leader there, is acceptable. But long-term leadership is needed to re-approach global affairs and achieve substantial results.

To Notice and For Improvement

There are very few positive African-American leaders to model in unmediated contemporary times for middle-aged male African, middle-class, educated, working adults like me. We need strong leadership representation from ourselves to our children to bridge the gap on minority education in the community and cre- ate new avenues to enhance African-American leadership.

Although past qualitative efforts to educate African Americans have increased, old-school efforts have made little feats to increase education competencies in the African-American community. In an article titled "Revisiting African-American Leadership," Ward points out: *"Our thinking about Black leadership for the 21st century must move beyond 20th-century models (Ward, 2007)."*

As an African-American leader, I intend to model a new-age leadership posture based on my education and experience, a new inclusive model, and a Christian servant leadership model. I want my children to see, experience, and adopt a servant posture that starts in the classroom and transforms them into their life expe- riences. I think for African-American children, in general, obtaining a superior education is nearly nonexistent due to social and economic barriers. As an African-American leader, I must prepare my children to participate in a world of inequality. Malcolm-Piqueux & Bensimon mention: *"The silver lining to this situation is that policy- makers and institutional leaders increasingly recognize the urgent need to focus their efforts and resources on creating equity in higher education (Piqueux & Bensimon, 2017, p.5)."*

I remember growing up in the public school system in the Philadelphia suburbs. Throughout my entire education, I was a minority. My children, too, are minorities in a similar environment and atmo- sphere. Speaking from experience, when students are minorities, an incongruence occurs, creating conflict. Minorities can have an introversion experience. The conflict may not be personal, but a level of understanding gets lost. A shift in focus from pro-education to un-education takes place. Concentration gets lost, and disruptive behaviors may become experienced. The education system spends countless hours mitigating and improving educational tools to prevent ineffective learning environments and to increase supportive instructional processes.

According to Bonner & Jennings:

> *"Some researchers posit that the dissonance that exists between school and student culture is the primary reason for the academic underachievement and social maladjustment of racially diverse students." (Bonner & Jennings, 2008, p.97)*

My son is an African American in a suburban vocational high school. My wife and I take an active role in his educational career. We try to get him the best education we can. He is the expected future of our family, along with our daughter. We advocate for him and his education. As a leader for him, I must lead and encourage; advance him along the way. Strayhorn makes an interesting point: *"Black male youth who persist through the early childhood education, middle school years, and make it through high school have other outcomes. For instance, still today, only 50% of Black males graduate from high school in the United States (Strayhorn, 2016, p.1107)."*

After high school, I went straight to college. I transferred in and out of a few schools before I had an "idea" about life. The first degree I earned belonged to a community college, where I finished in the top ten percent of the class. I earned my admission into the oldest International Honor Society. Phi Theta Kappa chose me to represent them as a leader in the community.

> *"Half of those who complete high school and attempt higher education begin at 2-year public community colleges, although many Black male high school graduates never attempt higher education (Strayhorn, 2016, p.1107)."*

After graduation from a community college, I continued my education at an elite four-year university. This time I was a minority at a private university. Thorough self-introspection from my educa- tion gave me a frame of reference for contentious issues I never knew existed. My four-year experience at an elite four-year school enabled me to successfully write my first book, "From My Mind From My Voice."

> *"A relatively small minority begin their postsecondary careers at 4-year colleges. And two-thirds of Black men who start college drop out before completing their degree, the highest attrition rate among both sexes and all races (Strayhorn, 2016, p.1108)."*

Few and far from the late African-American leadership model, control and exercise of power held limited legitimacy to only the middle and upper classes. Restricted power in African-American high society existed only amongst the educated and skilled. The lack of leadership in the African-American community for other African Americans lacks subsidies taking more of an effect on the education process and education system (Ward, 2007).

An African proverb challenged my ideology. The lesson from the proverb taught that a community could achieve substantial results more so than a worldly man.

"Blessed is the one who perseveres under trial because, having stood the test, that person will receive the crown of life that the Lord has promised to those who love him." (James 1:12)

"There is a new struggle requiring a new vision and leadership. African Americans have grown up in a world of Black millionaires and Black may-ors. They have seen Clarence Thomas, Colin Powell, and Condoleezza Rice on Television. For them, the promise of "Black faces in high places' rings hollow, and the call for "Black Unity"; a progressive idea in the late 1960', makes little sense in majority-Black cities and a nation where Black athletes, celebrities, and politicians can get seen everywhere (Ward, 2007)."

"So do not fear, for I am with you; do not be dis-mayed, for I am your God. I will strengthen you and help you; I will uphold you with my righteous right hand." (Isaiah 41:10)

There is a takeaway from the needed collective community of the past to the individual capitalist market society. African-American children lack community, especially in a monitorial setting. The popular media franchises, "The Superhero" and the "Do-It-Yourself" brand that American media markets so well.

James 1:12 tells us as leaders, the Crown of life is not received by idolizing Black millionaires. Life is not about "keeping up with the Joneses," instead of standing trial for God's Crown of Life. This Crown is worth far more than any earthly crown. The Lord has promised this Crown to those who love him. God is saying hope still exists for those who are not Black millionaires.

> *"For I know the plans I have for you," declares the Lord, "plans to prosper you and not to harm you, plans to give you hope and a future." (Jeremiah 29:11)*

> *African American leadership today has an essential role in shaping the radical revolution in core values we need to transform our world. African American leaders today cannot fight racism separate from the other struggles that confront us. They must project a vision of a transformed world and work with others to create a world in which we all can live to realize our full human potential. This initiative requires breaking out old patterns of thought and action to create new ones (Ward, 2007)."*

As an educated African-American servant leader, I must put my faith in the Lord so that he may provide harmony for togetherness in a global community. As a servant leader, I must realize that faith will eventually help the restorative process toward issues that confront my "identity," according to Amartya Sen.

There is a shift in the leadership paradigm into a critical, col- lective, and inclusive model. African-American leaders become challenged to envision a new reality with newer problems and systemic inequities. The authoritarian leadership posture needs to transition into a functional, operational, and healthy leadership discipline.

> *"You, dear children, are from God and have over-come them because the one who is in you is greater than the one who is in the world." (1 John 4:4)*

Bordas says, "When people respect each other and value differences, they can work together more amicably and productively " (Bordas, 2012, p.9)."

For African American-males to compete in education, the community must take responsibility and provide a more assertive African- American male representation of the African-American community. A future increase in African-American male democratic participation creates an opportunity for inclusiveness and integration.

> *"A knowledge base to inspire a core of multi-cultural leaders who recognize that diversity and inclusiveness are intrinsic to authentic and equitable democracy. These principles apply particularly to the Millennial Generation as more than 40 percent are Black, Latino, or American Indian, and many identify as mixed-race (Bordas, 2012, p.9)."*

Even advanced African-American students struggle with an ineffective education system. African-American leaders must take responsibility for supporting programs for gifted African-American stu- dents in their communities. As African-American leaders, we must exemplify experiences critical for teaching African-American students about coping mechanisms, disparities, and engaging. Bonner mentions:

> *"Without better alignment between cultural, gen- der, racial, and academic identity development, the typical outcome for the gifted African American male is often underachievement primarily associated with feelings of alienation and incongruence with the educational environment (Bonner, 2008, p.97).*

Some critical issues are facing African-American leadership in education. African-American leaders need to take responsibil- ity for the education of children in their communities. Still, there is a notion that the absence of African-American leadership repre- sentation in education has not changed for betterment in time but has decreased in authenticity. The gap in socio-economic privilege between middle-class and lower-class minority students makes supportive educational resources unavailable to the majority of the African-American community. Piquex & Bensimon argue that:

> *"Though it is true that racially minoritized and low-income students are more likely to enroll in some form of post-secondary education than in years past, their likelihood of completing a bachelor's degree once enrolled in college falls far below that of their white and economically privileged counterparts. The differences in college enrollment and college completion among historically marginalized and white and affluent populations have widened, suggesting that post-secondary education remains "separate and unequal" Clearly, American higher education has an equity problem (Piquex & Bensimon, 2017, p.5)."*

Instead of focused education solutions for African-Americans, a critical struggle for the African-American community, we are posited into non-educational media-based propagated lifestyles. In an edu- cated society, a student learns critical thinking, morals and ethics, world history, world cultures, reading and writing, the disciplines, and communication. But as African-Americans, we are manipulated and stereotyped as "animals" and "cheap labor." None say that African Americans can receive an education. Carter explicitly writes:

> *"Nowadays, in the imperialist western capitalist patriarch culture, most boys from poor and under-privileged classes are socialized via mass media and class-based education to believe that all that is required for their survival is the ability to do physical labor. Black boys, disproportionately numbered among the poor, have been socialized to believe that physical strength and stamina are all that matter. The socialization is as much in place in today's world as it was during slavery. Groomed to remain,*

permanent members of an underclass, groomed to be without choice and therefore ready to kill for the state in wars whenever needed, black males without class privilege have always been targeted for miseducation. They have been taught that "thinking" is not valuable labor and that "think- ing" will not help them survive. Tragically, many black males have not resisted this socialization. It is no accident that many brilliant-thinking black males end up imprisoned, for even as boys, they were deemed threatening, bad, and dangerous (Carter, 2010, p.46)."

We need to develop action plans and a new redirection for our children as a remedy for African-Americans to track progress in education. As African-American leaders, we need to evaluate the education of our community. Our leaders need to take evidence from our past, use a critical eye in our present, and create a plan of action for our future. Preskill explains this concept exceptionally well:

The first step in critical reflection. According to Preskill, "Those who engage in critical reflection must be prepared to confront how communities and organizations undermine justice; limit agency, con- centrate power in the few, and discourage individual and community renewal (Preskill, 2009, p.46)."

There are essential mainstreaming effects for the absence of African-American leadership in education amongst the African American community. Strayhorn states:

"Black males are more likely to be assigned to special education, suspended, or expelled from school (Strayhorn, 2016, p.1107)."

As African-American leaders, we need to create new avenues to encourage and support the education process for African-American children. Our children need to participate and find community in the school setting. Current efforts to allow safe identity searching are rudimentary and provide little support. The article "Capitalizing on Leadership Capacity" describes a situation:

> *"What can be problematic for the African American male who seeks to establish his racial identity in a school context is that these enclaves are ill-prepared to provide the necessary encouragement and space for this process to unfold. Additionally, as institu- tions, they are opposed to a developed sense of iden- tity that does not readily embrace all aspects of the Eurocentric frameworks upon which American edu- cation is based (Bonner, 2008, p.97)."*

Preskill suggests an alternative leadership posture to which the African American leadership model can subscribe. As a middle-aged African-American leader, I need to investigate my culture critically to shape my approach to improve and sup- port a path to education in my ethnic community. Preskill remarks:

> *"Developmental leadership targets the silenced and overlooked members of communities to help them find their voice and take a more active role in shaping their individual and collective destinies. Enthusiastically open to the contributions of others, especially those who have repeatedly been displaced and ignored by the majority (Preskill, 2009, p.8)."*

There are few positive African-American leaders to model in unmediated contemporary times for middle-aged, male, middle-class, educated, working African-Americans like me.

Although past qualitative efforts to educate African Americans have increased, old-school efforts have made little feats to increase education competencies in the African American community. As an African-American leader, I intend to model a new-age leadership posture based on my education and experience. Not just a new inclusive model but a Christian servant model of leadership. I want my children to see, experience, and adopt a servant posture that starts in the classroom and transforms them into their life experiences. The educational system spends countless hours mitigating and improving education tools to prevent ineffective learning environments and increases supportive instructional processes.

My son is an African-American male in a suburban vocation high school. My wife and I are very persistent with him in his educa- tional career. We advocate for him and his education. As a leader for him, I must lead and encourage him to advance along the way.

The first degree I earned belonged to a community college, where I finished in the top ten percent of the class. I earned my admission into the oldest International Honor Society. Phi Theta Kappa chose me to represent them as a leader in the community. Thorough self-introspection from my education gave me a frame of reference toward confrontational issues I never knew existed. My four-year experience at an elite four-year school enabled me to successfully write my first book, "From my Mind From my Voice." There is a takeaway from the needed collective community of the past to the individual capitalist market society today. African-American children lack com- munity, especially in a monitorial individualistic setting.

Although African American children turn to media culture, James 1:12 tells us as leaders, the Crown of life is not received by idolizing Black millionaires. Life is not about "keeping up with the Joneses," instead of standing trial for God's Crown of Life. This Crown is worth far more than any earthly crown.

I must put my faith in the Lord so that he may provide harmony for togetherness in a global community. As a servant leader, I must realize that faith will eventually help the restorative process toward issues that confront my "identity."

There is a shift in the leadership paradigm into a critical, col- lective, and inclusive model. African-American leaders become challenged to envision a new reality with newer problems and systemic inequities. For leadership to reeducate African-American communities, the authoritarian leadership posture needs to transition into a functional, operational, and healing leadership discipline.

For education reform to take place for African American males, the community must take responsibility and provide the desired leadership model. Even advanced African Americans students struggle with an ineffective education system. African American leaders must take responsibility for support programs for gifted African-American students in African-American communities.

African-American leaders need to take responsibility for the edu- cation of their children in their communities. The socio-economic privilege gap between middle-class and lower-class minority students makes supportive educational resources unavailable, primarily in the African-American community.

Instead of focused educational solutions for African Americans, we become misled into non-educational, media-based propagated lifestyles. Students learn critical thinking, morals and ethics, world history, world cultures, reading and writing, disciplines, and communication in an educated society. But as African Americans are manipulated and stereotyped as "animals" and "cheap labor."

We need to develop action plans for the future and a new direc- tion for our children to remedy African American progress in education. Our leaders need to take evidence from our past, use a critical eye in our present, and create a plan of action for our future. We must create new avenues to encourage and support the education process for our African-American children. Our children need to participate and find community in the school setting. Current efforts to allow safe identity-searching are rudimentary and provide very little support. African-American students need to explore their
ethnic identities openly to challenge contemporary thinking.

There are very few positive African-American leaders to model in unmediated contemporary times. Although past qualitative efforts to educate African Americans has increased, and old-school efforts have made little feats to increase education competencies in the African American community. This statement represents the sig- nificant components of this analysis. I address sporadic African- American leadership in education, then explain the lack of identity and provide evidence that African-American leadership needs a collective presence in the African American community.

Thought and critical-thinking statements toward African American leadership in education are clear and easy to follow. As an African-American leader, I intend to model a new-age leadership posture based on my education and experience. I want my chil- dren to see, experience, and adopt a servant posture that starts in the classroom and transforms them into their life experiences.

My son is an African-American male in a suburban vocation high school. My wife and I are very persistent with him in his edu- cational career. We advocate for him and his education. As a leader for him, I must lead, encourage, and advance him along the way. African-American children lack community, especially in a monitorial individualistic setting.

Although African American children are quick to emulate the media, James 1:12 tells us as leaders, the Crown of life is not received by idolizing Black millionaires. Life is not about "keeping up with the Joneses," instead of standing trial for God's Crown of Life. This Crown is worth far more than any earthly crown.

At least three significant points become identified clearly and linked to concepts. To educate African-American males in society, the community must take responsibility and provide a more assertive African American male representation of the African-American community. Even advanced African-American students struggle with an ineffective education system. African-American leaders must take responsibility for support programs for gifted African-American students in African-American communities.

Instead of focused education solutions for African Americans, we become posited into non-educational media-based propagated life- styles. In an educated society, a student learns critical thinking, mor- als and ethics, world history, world cultures, reading and writing, the disciplines, and communication. But as African Americans are manipulated and stereotyped as "animals" and "cheap labor." It is transparent that African Americans need more representation in the academic system.

The words used to describe the need for African-American lead- ership in our community illustrate the issue. The vocabulary draws the reader into a plea for African Americans to stand together, con- sult, and develop an action plan. This writing activity delivers a message that explains the problems and provides support for possible solutions. Overall, this expositional challenge allowed me to explore writing opacity, and improve my research capacity, orga- nization, reading, writing competency, and literary proficiency. I enjoyed this evaluation; I think I improved my critical analysis skills.

A New Call for Response

Consumers have the ultimate decision to purchase products and services from organizations they find official. This pur- chasing power can make or break an organization. Ethical marketing extracts values that incorporate honesty, fairness, and responsibility. Ethical, socially-responsible marketing campaigns can also demonstrate respect, transparency, and citizenship. Social marketing should "Do good not just to look good, but focus on being responsible and how your organization can truly help the community (Social Responsibility & Ethics in Marketing, 2018)." Socially responsible marketing should address "long-term effects and not short-term gains. Many organizations devalue ethical and social marketing. An ethical marketer should also whistle blow with the opportunity for the organization policy that does not reflect the ethical profile of the organization (Social Responsibility & Ethics in Marketing, 2018)". Socially responsible marketing observes the impact of marketing on a particularly collective society. For marketers to succeed with social responsibility, environmental challenges must get anticipated to adapt to societal values and beliefs change. Better socially-responsible organizations orient and market organization policy from a consumer perspective. Organizations can increase positive marketing outcomes by placing community value over profit value. As a result, customers are more inclined to pay a premium for the organization's products or services. An article provides a remarkable statement: "A company that uses ethical and socially responsible marketing strategy will gain the respect and trust of the customers they target and interact with (Social Responsibility & Ethics in Marketing, 2018)".

My Leadership Posture

My this "I believe" foci on listening skills, interpretation, resourcefulness, and faith have led me to my leadership beliefs. I can listen very well. I listen to all sides of the conflict before I engage in open dialogue. Listening is critical because it opens the floor for a deeper interpretation of problem-solving and answer-seeking. As a leader, I seek to empower co-workers with open discussion. When used, I instill strong interpretation skills and can help break down a problem for better clarity so that everyone can understand and contribute to the group or organization discussions. Owning my Christian clothing company has taught me to be resourceful. I must find materials that are concurrent, cost-effective, and high in quality. Resourcefulness provides a sense of awareness and adaptability. I need to be a successful steward in the Christian clothing community. My experience with faith has also taught me to lead with transformation. God transforms me to be a listener, to love, to act justly, to reason, to be in communion with, and to be a steward to transform my followers.

I learned Critical Reflection is very important to keep groups and organizations healthy. Although very difficult to achieve, Preskill states, critical reflection "involves making judgments about strengths and weaknesses taken to encourage group collaboration." When in process, "colleagues act freely and creatively." Most organizations shudder at this process because, under this system, critical reflection allows for open risk-taking and sometimes failure. But a true benefit occurs when a committed leader reflects critically and examines co-workers who are dissatisfied and disinterested.

Analyzing experience, I learned, is experience-centered and problem-based. "Each story is unique, some are similar, and some themes reoccur even through disparate experience." The point Preskill makes is that a learning process must occur and remain available for analyzing experience to work correctly. I agree when he says, "learning could not be meaningful or sustainable without basing it on real problems that arose from learners' daily experiences." This statement is compelling to my leadership beliefs. As Christians, we lack representation in contemporary world discussions. Everything in the media seems so secular in opinion. We need a strong Christian voice to delineate the truth from subjective opinion. I share similar leadership beliefs with analyzing experience. I believe problem-solving should be based upon "real life" problems or worldly top-down problems. In this case, social inequity, racism, and economic divide are problematic realities under which the "experience lens" should have a fundamental infusion and each particular experience or truth in the experience model.

CHAPTER

5

Charity & Christian Leadership

I n"TheSpiritualityofFundraising,"Ireflectuponfundraisingas a ministry discipline. This concept is most important to me, as Nouwen introduced thisidea.

Before religious identification and foundation, Nouwen touched upon the importance of fundraising:

> *"Henry's vision began with fundraising as a necessary but unpleasant activity to support spiritual things (Nouwen, 2004, p.iv)."*

Nouwen's leadership posture, relationship skills, and religious experience created a connected experience. Nouwen offers fundraising as spiritual as giving a sermon, entering a time of prayer,visitingthesick,or feedingthehungry.Fundraisingisaform of ministry and a way of announcing our vision and inviting others into our mission (Nouwen, 2004, p.3)."

Nouwen'sleadershipposturechallengesthenormsinsociety. With provensuccess,Nouwensuggests,fundraisingisacalltothe conversation. Fundraising as a ministry invites people to a new way of relating to their resources. By giving people a spiritual vision. We want them to experience a benefit by making their resources available to us (Nouwen, 2004, p.5)."

He also insightfully remarks that if our objectives are worthy of the declaration, others shall feel a sense of unity, involvement, and trust in fundraising for an organization. Nouwen states, "Fundraising is proclaiming what we believe in so that we offer other people an opportunity to participate with us in our vision and mission (Nouwen, 2004, p.iv)."

Again, Nouwen has a different interpretation of fundraising. He states, "Asking people for money is allowing them to put their resources at the disposal of the Kingdom (Nouwen, 2004, p.25)." In this context, I can become more passionate about my cause because I represent God's Kingdom.

I agree with the text's definition of Fundraising Basics towards Philanthropy and fundraising. The text states Philanthropy is the love of humankind usually expressed by an effort to enhance the well-being of humanity through personal acts of practical kindness or by the financial support of a cause or causes such as a charity, mutual aid or assistance, quality of life, and religion. Any effort to relieve human misery or suffering, improve the quality of life, encourage aid or assistance, or foster the preservation of values through gifts, services, or other voluntary action, any of which are external to government involvement or marketplace exchange (Ciconte, 2009, p.2)." This definition means more than just providing money and time offerings, this interpretation offers services of all the humanities. As I mature, I am more likely to accept the meaning of the text as a plausible, encompassing view of Philanthropy and fundraising.

I think those that fundraise are good people. They have a tough job raising funds to support their cause. I think many hours have contributed to making the process move smoothly. The more experience a fundraiser has, the stronger and more critical the organization will become over fund contributions. Time spent fundraising will make an organization more resourceful, and relationship-building for fundraisers and organizations is essential to non-profit organizations. On the other hand, I did not know the complete picture, for research reveals the most frequently important motivations for contributing to an organization. People participate because they believe in the cause or feel it is the right thing to do, and people think contribution will make an impact. People think money is becoming used as intended. People know someone who is affected or will be a beneficiary of the donation (Ciconte, 2009). I am not surprised that religious institutions remain the primary receivers, followed by educational institutions (Ciconte, 2009).

I think special events are my favorite method of fundraising. According to Fundraising Basics, "most people will attend special events to honor individuals, create publicity, or raise money for a cause (Ciconte, 2009, p.265)."

I am a people person who enjoys others in informal social settings and does well with these. I will most enjoy hosting a special event outside my organization's office. Whether for-profit or non-profit, special events are my cup of tea.

The four reasons to hold a special event fit my business model to optimize our fundraising capacity. I can highlight the Public's awareness of my organization. I can raise money to support my organization. I can focus attention on my organization's program. I can recruit for my organization using volunteer recognition and retention (Ciconte, 2009). Hosting special events seems to be my favorite method of fundraising.

Study the Rules

I created a startup company ten years ago. We sell Christian clothing: t-shirts, polo shirts, sweatshirts, and trademarked silver, gold, and platinum bullion. We are a structured corporation recog-
nized in the state of Pennsylvania. We have four officers, one director, and one owner. Our sales are not sustainable to support more staff, presently. According to Strategy Management Corp, our strategic planning begins with getting more exposure in the Christian retail market. As a brand, we want to observe other retailers and highlight market attributes that create success. Our brand will compete with other Christian brands through product sales and research. We want to develop our products and services to distinguish brand recognition from all others in the Christian retail market. As an organization, we will focus on researching product development toward the leading ten Christian clothing retailers in the market. We know that our bullion product is original and superior in quality today. Our resources are limited. We have a small operational and administrative budget. We do not owe loans. All the capital raised is from the personal owner and finances. We have an in-house inventory comprised of a few pieces. As our processes grow, we intend to streamline our in-house manufacturing assembly for clothing products. As an organization, we will make sure that we are

We are working toward common goals. Our sales and inventory are small, and our brand recognition is low, so our outcomes and results always need reassessment to change the market environment as we grow as an organization. We have an opportunity to create helpful planning. Not only can we adjust to market conditions, but we will take deliberate action to carry out strategic operations for rehearsed and intended results.

I read an interesting fact:

> *"Comparing the top 10 management tools over a ten-year period, strategic planning, benchmarking, outsourcing, our mission, and vision statements consistently remain in the top ten (The, p.1)."*

I am surprised that 74% spend more time on strategy development (The, p.2). I am not surprised that 62% of executives say strategy development is more complicated than a decade ago (The, p.2). There are many new organizations, business filing, and market saturation with the introduction of the internet. If I could agree with the summarized definition of strategic planning, I would agree with this text:

> *"Strategic planning is about asking and answering the right questions at the right time about the organization's current state and future direction (The, p.10)."*

I thought this concept was interesting, "Strategic planning helps organizations achieve two critical outcomes: clear decisions about purpose, strategy, and commitment to those decisions. It is a process designed to support leaders in being intentional rather than reactive (Allison, 2015, p.1)." An organization cannot waver or be partial to strategic planning. According to the text, "Strategic planning is systematic in that it calls for following a structured, driven process (Allison, 2015, p.1)." The distinction between strategy and planning differs from ideas to operational achievement. But strategic planning creates a synergy between ideas and creates methods to achieve them. "Strategy is aspirational in setting direction and is focused on broad, fundamental choices. Planning involves translating the strategy into concrete goals and guidance on achieving them (Allison, 2015, p.2p)." I find strategic planning important for my organization. Strategic planning can help my organization increase its impact and accomplish more of its mission by helping my leaders be intentional about priorities and proactive in motivating my organization to achieve them (Allison, 2015, p.3). I like this metaphor. "An organization's strategic plan is not an end, but rather is a means of achieving its purpose (Allison, 2015, p.17)." More than likely, I will reference this concept more than once. My organization will create a planning strategy like the description provided by the text.

"Strategic planning builds capacity in three ways: first, a clear direction supports the intentional use of resources, making the best use of capacity. Second, strategic planning often calls for investment in various dimensions of an organization's capacity, such as pro- gram evaluation, financial management, personnel training, or capital improvements. Third, strategic planning improves functioning. Strategic planning strengthens communication by building confidence in shared values and employing the entire organizational system to make the most important decisions (Allison, 2015, p.21)."

I am more interested in strategic planning. I read this form of preparation is increasing in importance. A recent survey suggests that there were intentions by more than 30% of the organizations surveyed to make greater use of strategic planning in 2015 when contrasted with 2014 (The, p.1). I want to learn about strategic planning practiced as a numerical and analytical process and as a creative process (The, p.5). I want to learn ways, required methods, procedures, and steps for an organization that needs synthesis around a shared vision that defines the purpose and direction of the business to practice strategic planning (The, p.6). I want to learn to create and implement a clarity of purpose to posit strategic decision-making (The, p.6). I want to learn our mission for strategic planning within my organization. Some organizations use it for fiscal planning. Some organizations use it for current performance and future needs. Others use it as a comprehensive exercise to plan five or more years (The, p.6). I want to learn the concept of strategic planning to be successful in the retail industry. From the reading, an organization that participates in the process must have a shared understanding of planned objectives (The, p.7). Furthermore, I want to seek methods to include directors within my organization.

I want to develop a leadership posture that is good at executing business strategies to create understanding, acceptance, and commitment toward organizational objectives (The, p.13). The retail environment and transaction process require strategy. The interactions involve choosing how best to respond to the circumstances of a dynamic environment. (Allison, 2015, p.1) I want to learn about building synergy and commitment. A developed plan without a synthesis of people, systems, and structures will not be successful. (Allison, 2015, p.1) I want to learn to create an emphasis on future strategic planning based on research that will lead to desired results. A developed plan helps my organization bring into focus our priorities, improves our processes, and pursues and orders our priorities (Allison, 2015, p.3).

For strategic planning to work for my organization, we must embrace change. My organization must have an ordinary under- standing of our sales and service objectives. To capitalize on market conditions, my corporation, at some point, should have a strategic plan. Our planning begins with getting the most exposure in the Christian retail market. As a brand, we want to compete with other Christian retailers and highlight market attributes that create success. Throughout product sales and research, our brand will outclass other Christian brands. We want to develop our products and services to distinguish our brand recognition from all others in the Christian retail market. As an organization, we will focus our energy on researching- ing product development toward the ten leading Christian clothing retailers in the market and offer our clothing and bullion products for completion. We should periodically check for new vendors and wholesalers that offer competitive pricing to drive down operational costs. Good accounting practices will also help us deal with change. Good use of balance sheets, income statements, and cash flow statements will help us run our organization efficiently. I think I am a sniff personality. If I catch wind of a new tool or niche market, I am all over it. I am like a fisherman in the sea. I am the type of person who does not only see the vast sea, but I know the sea as a vast world of opportunity. I see endless possibilities. I see hope. I understand the undiscovered and look for the discovered on my duty. I am a sniff. If someone catches bountiful seafood on an expedition, I envision that to be me. My eyes open wide, and my brain imagines heaven every time. Sniff is my personality toward business and life in general. I navigate from my shoulders, looking for new opportunities every time. I am always looking for the next bigger and better thing. Strategic thinking and change management get linked through priorities, resources, and employees with established common goals. Strategic thinking and change management are systemic. Both systems require synthesizing leaders and members and a commitment to collective organizational goals. Strategic thinking and change management deal with the response to changing business environments and methods to address them. Strategic thinking involves a plan that affects an organization. Change management is a metric that responds to the idea of an organization. Strategic thinking influences the effects of change management. Once a strategy goes active beyond a planning stage, change management involves a defensive or proactive risk management protocol to increase the outcome or accuracy of planned results. From a leadership perspective, change management requires understanding how organizations successfully experience change. Change management entails that organizational thinking gets embraced efficiently, adopted,

and deployed.

Empower the Public, Not Policy

Christian leaders can champion their teammates within their organizations. Christian leadership needs to operate as a change agent to deepen teammate learning and enhance the performance outcomes of their teammates by motivating, inspiring, and encouraging them. Christian leadership should foster learning with the acceptance of honest mistakes. Christian stewardship should provide conscious and intentional support for the goals and aspirations of their team members. Leadership should bestow a central platform to encourage decision-making across the common ground. Steward leadership should also conduct and facilitate dynamic feedback programming and offer motivational advice to accomplish concur- rent leadership team goals and objectives.

My point of view has changed throughout this course of study. I learned when to apply Christian leadership within my organization. Mary Virtue taught us that Christian leadership applies to various business processes and operations. My organization's leadership moments become infused with customer interaction, mentoring, business partnering organizations, and stakeholders. As focused as I may get, I must remember that I become challenged to get others to buy my vision. I must exemplify a steward of Jesus Christ in leadership when addressing the Public. We coin ourselves as a Christian organization; therefore, we must embrace our conduct and culture to reflect this posture.

Christian leadership has changed my behavior toward people management in my organization. According to lectures and PowerPoint presentations, our organization must create a positive culture. My organization should "Be an organization people want to work for (Virtue, 2019)." We need to find employees with the right fit, prepare them for success, and promote and reward them for suitable performance and retainable results.

I propose to use Stewardship leadership skills of motivation, inspiration, and encouragement for personal development throughout my on-the-job learning experience. My leadership skill development and our organization's operation plan will help focus on highlighting our mission, vision, and values statements to maintain our corporate culture. Based upon the Butler & Waldroop text, I will include my embedded interests, also, to support personal fulfillment.

I will conduct a Swot analysis for a progressive action plan. I will develop a leadership journal or portfolio to detail my experience and provide insight into my leadership challenge. I will attempt to practice active feedback with stakeholders to achieve goals and, with these performance metrics, set new intelligent objectives. I will evaluate my progress every four to six months with a SWOT analysis. I shall develop our new goals as needed. Once an objective gets completed, I will document the outcome, provide feedback, and create another smart objective based upon our mission, vision, and values of our organization operations.

According to reflexive notes, implementing these behavior changes of motivation, inspira- tion, and encouragement will cultivate great talent, benefit from diversity, and instill job gratification (Virtue, 2019). Knowing these leadership behaviors, I have selected two scripture verses for faith.

Scripture has taught, "He guides the humble in what is right and teaches them his way. All the ways of the LORD are loving and faithful toward those who keep the demands of his covenant (Psalms

25:9-10)." Strong Christian leaders motivate their teammates in positive cultures. Again, I want my organization to "Be an organization people want to work for (Virtue, 2019)." My leadership posture stems from our mission, vision, and values statement, and each culture statement in our organization reflects an aspect of steward leadership. Our organization statements and "Teach them his way" follow Psalms 25:9-10. My organization builds its authenticity by aligning its values with biblical scripture, organizational faith, and personal faith.

As a part of my faith, I learned from scripture, "I will instruct you and teach you in the way you should go; I will counsel you with my loving eye on you (Psalms 32:8)." Psalms 32:8 is exemplary: organizations, we do not know the way, and we can only prepare and react to the change in market conditions. My leadership posture needs to reflect the scripture to adapt to market change. I embrace this verse in faith, not knowing the future of my organization.

The Best Model

In my opinion, human behavior gets taught, learned, and repeated. I believe the nature of people is collectively good. Scripture states that we became created in God's image, and God's creation is good. Satisfaction, or relational connecting to achieve wholeness with physical, emotional, mental, a n d spiritual well-being, motivates human behavior. Breakdown in bonding or relationship wholeness, whether physical, emotional, mental, or spiritual, causes friction, acts as a demotivator, and discourages positive, constructive behaviors. The manager's role in working with the staff is to achieve and deliver objectives set forth by leadership, to motivate staff to complete and carry out specific tasks and operational
functions of the organization.

I am a teamwork-oriented person. I like open communication, and I like to listen to the opinions of others. I value the opinion of others more than my own. I encourage establishing common ground and tapping into shared intelligence. I appreciate working in groups with diversity. Communities are evolving and require a new approach to problem-solving that includes various types of people with different backgrounds. A strength I have is the experience of working with diverse groups of team members. However, I feel that I need to gain experience with managing organization members in an entry-level setting.

I am good at creating strategies and developing a vision. I established a Christian clothing brand that focuses on biblical verse 2 Timothy 2:15. The brand's mission is to develop a movement that expresses that hard work and perseverance can empower families, communities, and societies. We want to put our brand on every person who understands love and achievement are successive and Godly. As a result, the company operates as a registered Pennsylvania C-Corporation with partnering web promotions, with at least two trendy solicitations and one major promoter.

I would have difficulty working with pol- icy-driven management versus public-oriented management. I have worked for companies that post the "at will" employer in their policy. Companies that care about their by-laws more than the "condition" of their employees. I have never been a fan of these organizations. I care about the welfare of my workers, and I want my organization's culture to embody par- ticular principles that develop human resources.

Embrace and Replenish Resources

Y unus bluntly remarks, "Ninety-four percent of the world income goes to 40 percent of the people, while the other 60 percent must live on only 6 percent of the world income. Half of the world lives on two dollars a day or less, while almost a billion people live on less than one dollar daily (Yunus, 2009, p.3)." Given these facts alone, we as a global society require social entrepreneurs and social businesses to examine the gaps in the community fabric of our global population to then address the systemic social issues and take social responsibility.

Social entrepreneurship creates an equilibrium change when traditional change models do not fit the social responsibility in either big business models or government initiatives. Social entrepreneurs may use social business to develop, fund, and implement solutions to social, cultural, or environmental issues. Social entrepreneurs typically attempt to broaden further social, cultural, and environmental goals for social issues (Social entrepreneurship, 2018). The results for social entrepreneurs amount to social transformation. Martin & Osberg posit that "Social transformation is positive fundamental and lasting change to the prevailing conditions under which most members of society live and work. Individuals and groups aim for the status quo, attempting to shift it to a new superior state (Martin & Osberg, 2015, p.32)."

Yunus remarks that governments can actively and responsibly participate in addressing social problems, and the sheer size and capacity of the government can assemble resources readitarily (Yunus, 2009). Alongside government participation, business impact investors are vital for social transformation. Eggers & Macmillian claim business investors "can massively increase the number of lives touched by concentrating investments in specific industry sectors in specific geographies and by investing in a range of organizations to accelerate the development of these industry segments (Eggers & Macmillian, 2013 p.220)." When government and businesses participate in social responsibility with organizations of the same social issue, industry load advancement, and effective group time management occur to scale the government and business model toward the collective of those particular social issues (Eggers & Macmillian, 2013).

Social entrepreneurs should develop and establish conditions for market rules and controls to protect the interest of the poor and marginalized (Yunus, 2009, p.5). Social entrepreneurs, most importantly, should attempt to shift the social equilibrium by systemically changing and advancing unfair and unaddressed social conditions (Martin & Osberg, 2015). Addressing social responsibility for organizations and social entrepreneurs requires a focus on social benefits than profit maximization. Social benefits are becoming more critical. Poverty reduction, social justice, and world hunger move to the forefront of social entrepreneurship and alleviate social issues instead of substantiation for financial reward (Yunus, 2009, p.28). An essential aspect of social entrepreneurship for alleviating poverty predicates profit businesses owned by the poor and marginalized. The social benefit occurs when the dividends and equity growth generated by the organization will benefit themselves and the poor. As a result, the dividends will help them climb and lessen their way from poverty-stricken socio-economic status (Yunus, 2009).

The main idea from Getting Beyond Better is that social entrepreneurs must understand the world they wish to change, envision a new future, build a change model, and scale a new solution. When entrepreneurs understand the world they want to change, they must champion many tensions: abhorrence, appreciation, expertise and apprenticeship, and experimentation and commitment. These actions improve society by creating an equilibrium shift. The marginalized become empowered and become less impoverished with the capacity of self-efficacy.

Social entrepreneurs envision a new future when they develop clear and comprehensive knowledge about social issues they intend to change. They must evaluate and understand social issues and describe the vision of impact on social business efforts. A social entrepreneur must have a bright vision of the impact on social issues and definitive steps to achieve social impact for change to work effectively (Martin & Osberg, 2015).

Social entrepreneurs use a building change model to guide their vision. The model acts as a blueprint for the social entrepreneur's vision and the social issue's change impact. The model is a map and explicit direction to influence change, which results in impact change (Martin & Osberg, 2015). To scale their operations, social entrepreneurs must operate as an open-source and encourage others to join and build their model on a community platform. Social entrepreneurs rally others in the community for help rather than take a self-serving approach. Social entrepreneurs that have the most scale of impact make several decisions toward social issues for social business. They do not sit around waiting; they are heavily active in the social community (Martin & Osberg, 2015).

The main idea from the Solution Revolution is each wave-maker has a position in a solution economy. According to Eggers & Macmillian, "wavemakers do more than dent the problems society faces. They change the battlefield on which people face problems (Eggers & Macmillian, 2013, p.19)." Wavemakers include investors and conveyors, multinationals, innovators, steady suppliers, and citizen changemakers (Eggers & Macmillian, 2013). The theory of a solution economy intends for wavemakers to work systemically together to maximize resources by addressing, changing, and scaling the impact on social issues by a repetitious method. If the system is used correctly, social issues become broken down in an orderly fashion. The solution economy process and theory aim to improve societal health through social entrepreneurship and social business via wave-maker participation.

Under the scope of change impact, investors and conveyors comprise venture philanthropists and impact investors who gather investment returns for a social application. Any dividend or financial gain earned gets reinvested for social benefit (Eggers & Macmillian, 2013, p.21). Multinationals embrace the double bottom line and maximize profit while advancing social impact, and this has become the new trend for growing organizations (Eggers & Macmillian, 2013, p.29). The innovators blend profitability and social responsibility. They find an area for innovation and provide products and services that fulfill unmet needs (Eggers & Macmillian, 2013, p.35). Steady suppliers are organizations that deliver services on behalf of the government (Eggers & Macmillian, 2013). Citizen Changemakers comprises volunteers who collaboratively contribute to public benefit and are often empowered by social entrepreneurs to help with innovative market technologies (Eggers & Macmillian, 2013).

The main idea of Creating a World Without Poverty states that governments and social businesses can substantially remedy social issues with legislation and funding otherwise unattainable. Social business has become a recent competitor to profit-making businesses. The introduction and prevalence of social businesses improve society more now than in the past. Social organizations are trending in the movement for social responsibility, especially in the for-profit sector. As a result, business contributions outweigh any government-supported financial assistance to date. Social entrepreneurs and businesses are making the business market aware that social issues can get addressed in traditional business environments. Social issues are no longer a government duty. Business organizations, such as social businesses, are handling social responsibility more and more, causing the business world to address and refocus attention toward social responsibility. As more social entrepreneurs make a profit and social impact, businesses become forced to refocus their business practices to compete in contemporary market environments.

As a global society, we require social entrepreneurs and businesses to examine the gaps in the community fabric of our global population. Social entrepreneurs and businesses can address systemic social issues and take social responsibility. We should not stop until social entrepreneurs understand the world they wish to change, envision a new future, build a change model, and scale a new solution. **The implementation of** a solution economy process for wavemakers to work together maximizes resources by addressing, changing, and scaling the impact on our social issues and establishing a scalable change impact. Nevertheless, governments and social business input can substantially remedy social issues with legislation and funding otherwise unattainable.

Contemporary Leadership

L eadership can get defined as delivering a group or organization to an objective, goal, or project to an end. Leadership "is the art and practice of guiding a person or group from where they

are toward the greater competence and fulfillment they desire (Schamber, 2003)." Strong leaders are compassionate, good listeners, community-driven, and pioneering. Leadership needs to shape the needs, ideas, and goals of the group or organization's majority to be successful. "True leadership emerges from those whose primary motivation is a deep desire to help others (Spears, 2005, p.2)." Today's leadership must encompass a diverse population, or heterogeneous mixture, of races, cultures, and ethnicities. "Leadership is not about problems and decisions; it is a profoundly relational enterprise that seeks to motivate people toward a vision that will require significant change and risk on everyone's part. Decisions are simply the doors leaders and followers walk through to get to the land where redemption can get found (Allender, 2006, p.14)." A good leadership model examines the successful attributes of other strong leaders in other regions to incorporate similar value practices into various leadership models. More than ever, there is a need for a global leadership model due to the change in the global community. "A better leadership model shapes, alter and elevates the motives and values and goals of their followers (Wren, 1995, p.103)." A healthy leadership posture focuses on "setting and reaching goals, as well as overcoming obstacles, problem-solving, generating options, and finding solutions (Schamber, 2003)." Strong leadership models and leaders must get established in groups and organizations where corruption and organizational structure have collapsed.

Effective leadership delivers a group or organization's objectives, goals, or results—effective leadership by coaching "evok- ing excellence in others (Schamber, 2003). Basic leadership intends to make ideas into objectives. "Effective Leaders provide groups with structure; goals; and instruments to achieve goals (Kellerman, 2008, p.59)." Effective leaders use education and experience to guide and direct group and organization members toward visionary objectives. Critical leadership aims to teach group and organization members to train and transform non-leaders to lead. "Transforming leadership changes some of those who follow into people whom others may follow in time (Wren, 2005, p.103)." This leadership creates a model of sustainability. A new leader must emerge when a leader leaves to carry on a group or organization function. A critical leader must develop the roles, skills, characters, and attributes of the group members for the best approach to the group or organizational problem-solving. Transforming leadership "occurs when one or more persons engage with others in such a way that leaders and followers raise one another to higher levels of motivation and morality." (Kellerman, 2008, p.67). Traditional leadership models ignore the group's ideas or the organizational development and emphasize individualism, meritocracy, free-market, and competition. As a result, the need for character-based leadership gets lost in government and business organizations. Effective leadership aims to liberate groups and organizations from reoccurring problems based on experience to achieve a targeted result. Critical leadership is restorative and continuous. Effective leadership aims to provide order for a group or an organization. With a growing mixed population within the United States, leadership today calls for a new inclusive leadership model in government and business groups and organizations. An inclusive leader must, at least, develop skills and the characters of the group and organization members for a sound approach (Preskill, 2009).

As an emerging leader, I wish to develop more vital and effective leadership qualities in character for decision making, commu- nity-based involvement, and re-teaching leadership and leadership consistency. A moral leader develops a stronger character, and a moral leader acts in faith for a just character. Despite race, religion, ethnicity, or cultural differences, a leader must learn to be sensitive to all forms of human life for the greater good (Bordas, 2012). Critical leaders are influential and moral rather than ineffective and immoral.

A strong leader needs to make decisions based on the total picture, not from materialistic, individual, or capitalistic wants, but the needs of the less heard and the heart of society. "Emerging leaders shall protect the welfare of individuals in society and ensure fair treatment of all people (Ng, 2011, p.43)." Leaders empower global social reform and global economic expansion, then offer the luxuries of western culture to the subsisting world and the global consumer (Bordas, 2012). Influential leaders place more concern on social justice than institutional justice.

An inclusive leader is a community leader. New and "transformational leaders shall take actions consistent with inclusivity and social responsibility (Ng, 2011, p.43)." The United States is a heterogeneous community, and therefore, the United States needs heterogeneous, "democratic republic community" leaders to encompass future community global leadership models today. "Emerging leaders need more concern for social justice (Ng, 2011, p. 43)." Diversity of backgrounds is so disparate that leaders must be sensitive to innate differences (Bordas, 2012). Influential leaders address fol- lowers in the communities that they serve.

The best leadership models need replenishment, "the best of the best." Education removes the source of ignorance. A well-coached leader is a relationship of unconditional acceptance where learning, performance, growth, and change naturally occur. (Coaching). Re-teaching superior leadership bestows superior leaders. Get strong leaders in various disciplines to educate the population. After so much turnover, strong leadership models will supersede pastmediocre leadership. This leadership will strengthen the leadership community as a whole. Effective leaders learn from their followers as much as other leaders. Continuing education for leaders will remain vital for new ideas and innovation for effective leaders.

Not only do leaders need these qualities, but they need these consistently. Good leadership needs continuity and less sparsity. A leader here or there is exemplary, but long-term leadership is needed to re-approach global affairs to achieve substantial results. Effective leadership requires coverage and frequency, and accountable and available leaders become a foundation for the discovery process.

As a leader, I am a good listener. I have a good rapport, and I always find a way to see the good in people, regardless of whether they are wrong. I approach situations with neutrality and truly under- stand all-party points of view before speaking. I show the speaker the commitment they require and am not opinionated, giving the speaker authority to explain themselves.

My plan to build on my listening skills is to encourage open discussion. I will engage in active listening by confirming the speaker and allowing the speaker to voice their opinions without judgment or ridicule. I will try to ensure everyone in the group listens to each other and that everyone's opinion matters.

I am very empathetic and always see the positive in people. I relate well to others and accept others for who they are. I will try to get to know someone as best as I can. I will try to break down barriers that prohibit communication and create bias. I want to learn about people who are different than me and listen to stories of culture and history that can influence my life and my family.

I have healing qualities and tend to feel sympathetic and supportive of the victims and the oppressed in society. I plan to continue participating in the shelter ministry by serving the community with home-cooked meals for homeless and street-bound people during the holidays. Working in the community is another way to offer my services outside my Church and home.

I am aware of others; I see the whole picture with people. I try to look for the best outcome. I will try to be more helpful to those

whoneedhelp.Asapartofmyleadership,Iwillassistmyco-workers withahelping hand.IfIseeaneedforhelp,Iwilloffermyservices. IfallshortofGod'sgloryfor stewardship.Itrytoprotectmy family;Itrytobeacompanionwithfriends;I trytolovemydog;I trytoattendChurch;ItrytofearGod,andItrytobeamanof Christ. Ihaveasenseofprovision;whetherathome,Church,work,school, or servingothers,Ihaveaplacetogiveback.Ialsocontinuallyprovidetithe,gifts, andofferingstopracticemyfaith. Idonottake advantage of work. I am loyal to my employer and committedtomywork. Iamwillingtoopenmyeyesand heartto otherpersonsofGod.IwilltreatGod'speopleasiftheywerepeople ofmy own. I will be less critical ofthose I love and more critical ofmyself towards those I do not know. God has entrusted me with hislove and provision, and I think I need to share it with those who
need it the most.

Commitment to growth is ongoing, and I offermy daughter library books and academic journals to study. I reward both mysonandmydaughterfor homeboundchores.Weholdfamily meetings for current events and community discussions. I want to pursue a learning environment for my family and create an open discussion abouteducation,religion,politics,etc. Just topics to explore, thought to evoke emotion and understanding.

Ihaveagoodstartinbuildingacommunity. Inthecommunity,I volunteerwithchurchministriesandshelters,havepublished a Christian book, anddonatemonthlytoaChristianministry to saveanAfricanChildoverseas.I haveastrongsenseofcommunity: I develop relationships in workplaces that establish heartiness. Every company I worked for had a "home away from home" culture and an open-doorpolicy. I have trust in the purpose of moving the community forward. My superiors have only said good statements about me. When I enter rooms, calmness follows, and I am slow to judgepeople.

Iwillcontinuemyministriestobuilduponmystrengthas a transformationalleader. I will continue establishingworkingrelationships at work,athome,andpublic. Eventually, I plan to

participate in more community activities as my children grow older. I want to practice servant leadership posture more often in the process. However, I lack awareness. I am too focused on getting my job done and not aware of the workplace formalities, normalities and
particulates of my co-workers and superiors.

I need to pay more attention to my surroundings. I need to observe my workplace and learn everyone's likes and dislikes. I need to learn about others' frustrations and pleasures. I must learn the values and ideas that please the supervisor and co-workers.

I fall short of Conceptualization, and I find it hard to see the possibilities for scenarios to go wrong and methods to remedy them. I need a mentor to help identify and provide feedback on problem-solving and management issues. I have a problem hurting people's feelings and want everyone to feel valued.

I lack managerial experience because I do not know the best-fit personnel places. I need mentoring to maximize workforce efficiency and productivity. I do not know employees' motivations and am just learning leadership models with no leadership expertise.

I am persuasive, but I need help. I do not present all the facts before I try to convince others to buy into my ideas. I need to be more factual, with examples rather than word of mouth. I never have the appropriate documentation to persuade my followers.

I tend to say one thing knowing the truth is something else by the negligence of not seeking the truth. I give the "ballpark" answer when the exact answer is needed. I often do this when I want someone to let me do the work on my own. I mean no harm, but I do not consider others' time and efforts to process the same information. Instead of getting the proper documentation, I will certify information without legitimacy. When I provide incorrect information, I create inaccuracies and more work than needed.

Drawn to Leadership

I intend to reference critical points of the book that highlight and connect to leadership experiences that I can draw from. Although my experience is limited, I provided working examples critical to my leadership model that shaped my perspective and continue to add dimension to my posture. I have provided highlights and quotes where my experience can extract meaning and purpose from reading Unleader.

One key point Overstreet expresses is, "But it will probably have to be one of you. Because who besides a follower of Jesus could hope to have the character and integrity necessary to withstand the pressure of corruption long enough to bring lasting change?" (Overstreet, P.2)

I had work experience that challenged my character and my integrity. Corrupt management was stealing files from their company and giving them to another company. The management asked me to steal them, and I told them this was stealing and I did not feel comfortable doing so. I asked Jesus to intervene in the situation and to give me the strength to fight the pressure of corruption.

Overstreet says, "And what about you? What would your leadership look like if you were suddenly handed more power?" (Overstreet, P.2)

During my service in the military, I received an opportunity to be in the rope program, and I earned a white rope for chapel services. As a part of the program and its status, the program appoints special powers for "ropes" over military personnel. As a "rope," a servicemen rope has special duties and powers to assist, account for, direct, organize, and lead military personnel on duty. My rope powers became appointed through the chapel ministries program. I felt I had a calling to help the Church while serving my country. Selecting the Church for stewardship in the service became one of my experiences with servant leadership.

Again, "Would your leadership be an example of righteousness and justice, or would you give in to the temptations that power always presents? A simple way to answer that question is to evaluate what your leadership looks like right now." (Overstreet, P.2)

While working for a company, the manager would cut corners by falsely accounting for product inventory, although he had no idea. When I was a worker, the leadership setup was authoritarian. I said, "Look, I think you might want to count all those items for at least one purpose; trouble may come back to you." He looked at me and told me, "Whatever." I told him, "If we are going to stay out of trouble, we will have to work together and do the best we can to get management off our backs." He gave me a look implying that he was better than me. Then he told me, "Whatever, man." In this situation, I tried to act with righteousness and justice. I identified the issue that, together as a unit, we were creating a company problem. I had to absolve the problem and try to recommend a solution. Instead of pointing a finger, I used a group approach. Despite the results, I think he knew we had a problem.

Overstreet proclaims, "God's values also go against our human nature. Justice, goodness, dying to self, humility-none of these come naturally to us. That is why becoming a leader who pleases God and brings him joy is impossible apart from our growth in relationship with God." (Overstreet, P.3)

Before I became baptized, I did not have a strong relationship with God. I did well, but I felt inadequate and empty. I especially felt unholy in high school. I always did great in school: ten honors courses, three sports a year, five extra-curricular activities, a job, a girlfriend, and friends. Yet I still felt alone. I was miserable. I always passed off advancing my relationship with God until after I graduated. Nothing I completed was good enough. I had to have the most remarkable thing. Where I lived was not friendly enough. The car I drove was too poor. The grades I received were not high enough. My SAT score was not great enough. Looking back, I see it is impossible to grow into a just relationship with Him while living against His ways. My life changed in 2003. This change is the year I gave my life to Christ. I began to change inside out. I began to worry less about worldly pleasures and focus on a relationship with Him. I began to become more people-oriented and less materialistic. I began to become more morally conscious and less oblivious. I became involved in the community and the Church. I became less of a number and became more of a person. I began to develop, and Christ in me became awesome. I learned about justice, and I learned about humility. I learned to develop a character. I found God's values go against our human nature.

I observed, "People have been self-centered, focused on their interests and reputations, and living in fear of authority ever since sin entered the world. Therefore, real stories about real leaders from any era and any culture are relevant to us today." (Overstreet, P.5)

As a father, I must teach my kids to be cross-cultural from all walks of life. My children are biracial. Not only do they need acceptance, but they need to accept others. Today, we live in a society where successful leaders can communicate, teach, and respond to national and global markets to conduct business and politics for local, national, and global communities. Schools are becoming more diverse, and communities are becoming more populated. More and different groups of people are sharing resources. I want my children to learn and apply their education to help their families prosper and, at best, join the global conversation and participate as nation-state contributors.

Overstreet states, "Righteous leadership results in people grow- ing into their potential." (Overstreet, P.54)

Throughout my working career, I have been laid off several times and fired. Within the past eight years, I have created a "startup" company to my success. I have written a book and have many impressive academic achievements. Besides my company, I have few work experiences calling me a "manager" or "leader." Within the past week, after an important meeting with Veteran Affairs, they approved sponsorship to help me grow my company. They found that I am at a disadvantage in the workforce because I am a disabled veteran, and they will support me with self-employment. Working for companies who treat me unjustly as a "disabled veteran" and starting my own company in the interim is an opportunity for professional help that presented itself. In light of several bad work experiences and choices, Veteran Affairs took a chance on me. I am more self-employed and am growing to my potential with help from Veteran Affairs.

Overstreet mentions, "Denial and excuses were all that Samuel got from Saul the second time he was confronted with the facts. How often do we justify our disobedience to ourselves, others, and even God when we know we have fallen short?" (Overstreet, P. 61)

I find this very true about our church attendance. We missed the entire Church this summer because we made some "obligations" outside the Church. We sat by the pool or went to the beach for the summer. We made excuses not to attend Church because it was "summertime." For some families, this is reasonable. For us, this was disobedient. We knew we were wrong. Every Sunday, ten-thirty rolled around, and everyone in the house became silenced. One of our children would speak up. Are we going to Church today? My wife and I would grimace, "No! We are going to sit by the pool!" Then, my wife and I would look at each other and say, "We are going once summer is over!" Then, we would look at the ceiling as if we were Adam and Eve and had eaten the forbidden fruit. This moment is a classic example of my family falling short. We have been tithing our ten percent as requested by the Christian faith. But our community fellowship and ministry involvement have suffered. Time in and time out, I try to justify the absence of my church participation. At one time, I praticed the men's ministry, then I quit because I thought the ministry took too much of my time away from my family. Currently, we participate in International Christian Ministries, a ministry that helps children in Africa get the resources they need to survive and function. I just about wanted to quit that, but I told myself God does not like ugly. I am trying to make the point that my wife and I have to be consistent. We are leading children on whom we make impressions. Scripture states, "Train up a child in the way he should go, and when he is old, he will not depart from it." (Proverbs 22:6). Even when we are not paying attention, someone is. God knows we fall short. Although disobedient, God knows our hearts in scripture, faith, and practice.

Overstreet explains, "Leaders who love and serve those they lead engender those emotions in others. It is quite simple if you want to know how to earn the love of those you work together. I love them first. It is what God with us." (Overstreet, P.100)

My son, Cayden, now 18, has made remarkable progress. The road has been rough. I learned when young Cayden struggled because of his autism. In kindergarten, we noticed his social dysfunction. He struggled with social interaction. One time we had to remove Cayden from daycare because of his inability to communicate the accident he had, and the daycare could not communicate with him, so we removed him. Throughout his elementary years' situations occurred. I remember someone bullied him on the bus, and his coat stolen. The other kids would overpower him because Cayden did not have the social skills to communicate and defend himself. We spent hours in meetings, creating a treatment plan for Cayden and learning coping mechanisms to use throughout his life. We even utilized community-based services: wrap-around (TSS) and mobile therapy. Cayden worked hard in school. In middle school, we continued services for Cayden. He earned the Presidential Scholastic Achievement Award for the most consecutive honor roll marking periods in middle school, along with a few other middle schoolers. Cayden is currently in high school, participating in his individualized education plan. He is interested in the automotive discipline and wants to pursue and further his education.

Overstreet references, "Do I lead from the security of knowing God's love?" (Overstreet,P.101)

In July 2016, my wife and I decided to sell our home. On the market, our house sold in a few hours. We picked out a home we liked in Owen J School District. As part of our home sale, we needed a contingency to finalize our sale. We applied for a pre-approval letter for the home in Owen J. The homeowner in Owen J said he would wait one week until the pre-approval letter became issued. Well, he did not wait. He undercut us and sold the house to another family. We were out of a house, and our house was off the market. Later that month, I get laid off from my job. The same company tells me that they no longer need my services. Now, I am going to a new home with no job and no home to fall back on. A few weeks later go by. We find a new home and a new mortgage broker. We get a pre-approval letter, and God is ultimately blessing us. Our house sells, and we move out; however, we do not close on the new home until September 2016. So, we ask if we can rent our home for a month before we close. The homeowner approves.

No one occupied the home, so they said why not. Then came the next roadblock. The mortgage broker says he cannot do the loan. Then we moved into our new home. Closing was scheduled for September. We had nowhere to go and no loan approval. They gave us a pre-approval letter, but they gave us no loan. I had no job and no home. I had to lead by knowing God's love. Our phones were ringing nonstop. We get a phone call from the homeowner's realtor. She says we have someone who can help you. We were so desperate that we asked anyone to help us out of this situation. God delivered. She was the sweetest lady and explained we did everything right but had met a junk broker. He recommended procedures she would never ask us to do. She delivered our loan on October 31, 2016. God's love delivered us from a reached situation to show us that he is always with us. "Trust in the Lord with all your heart. Do not depend on your understanding. Seek his will in all you do, and he will show you what path to take." (Proverbs 3:5)

Finally, Overstreet writes, "All he wants us to do is grow in our acceptance and understanding of his love for us and respond appropriately. When our leadership becomes based on the security of being loved, almost everything else comes into proper perspective. Competition fades away because we do not need to compete. Jealousy, strife, and anger cease. Fear, with its ugly tentacles gripping our hearts of hearts, dissolves as perfect love casts out fear." (Overstreet, P.102)

My relationship with my wife is built with God at the head of our relationship. We are rooted in our faith and treat each other with acceptance and understanding that God is with us both. I treat my wife as a child of God. She is exceptional, and I am a steward for her. She is God's child, and me just a provisionary for her in our relationship with God. When we experience God's love for one another, we find more profound respect and love for each other. We are an example to our children to lead with a love for God first, for self, and for each other. We spend time together in fellowship and with those who love us.

To this end, I referenced critical points of the book that highlighted and connected my leadership experiences. I provided working examples critical to my leadership model that shapes my perspective and continue to add dimension to my posture. I have provided highlights and quotes where my experience can extract meaning and purpose from the reading. I leave with a quote, "A leader knows the way, goes the way, and shows the way." John C. Maxwell

WORKS CITED

Allison, M., & Kaye, J. (2015). *Strategic planning for nonprofit orga-nizations: a practical guide and workbook.* Hoboken: John Wiley & Sons.

BibleGateway. (n.d.). Retrieved November 13, 2017, from http://www.biblegateway.com/

Bonner, F. A., Jennings, M. E., Marbley, A. F., & Brown, L. (2008). Capitalizing on Leadership Capacity: Gifted African American Males in High School. *Roeper Review, 30*(2), 93-103. doi:10.1080/02783190801954965

Bordas, J. (2012). *Salsa, soul, and spirit: leadership for a multicultural age:.* San Francisco, CA: Berrett-Koehler.

C. (2014). The Newly Black Americans. *Transition,* (113), 52. doi:10.2979/transition.113.52

Carter, D. (2010). A Nonracial Education: On Navigating Diaspora, Anti-Black Caricature, and Anthropology. In *Navigating the African Diaspora: The Anthropology of Invisibility* (pp. 35-70). University of Minnesota Press. Retrieved from http://ezproxy.eastern.edu:2076/stable/10.5749/j.ctttjm0.6

Ciconte, B. L., & Jacob, J. G. (2009). *Fundraising basics: a complete guide.* Sudbury, MA: Toronto.

Eggers, W. D., & MacMillan, P. (2013). *The solution revolution: How business, government, and social enterprises are teaming up to solve societys toughest problems.* Boston: Harvard Business Review Press.

Malcom-Piqueux, L., & Bensimon, E. M. (2017). Taking Equity- Minded Action to Close Equity Gaps. *Peer Review AAC&U*. Retrieved October, 2017.

Martin, R. L., & Osberg, S. R. (2015). *Getting beyond better: How social entrepreneurship works*. Boston, MA: Harvard Business Review Press.

Nouwen, H. J. (2004). *The spirituality of fund-raising*. Nashville, TN: Upper Room Ministries.

Overstreet, J. (2011). *Unleader: the surprising qualities of a valuable leader*. Downers Grove, Ill: IVP Books.

Preskill, S., & Brookfield, S. D. (2009). *Learning as a way of lead- ing: lessons from the struggle for social justice*. San Francisco, CA: Jossey-Bass.

Social entrepreneurship. (2018, November 13). Retrieved from https://en.wikipedia.org/wiki/Social_entrepreneurship

Strayhorn, T. L. (2016). Factors That Influence the Persistence and Success of Black Men in Urban Public Universities. *Urban Education,52*(9),1106-1128.doi:10.1177/0042085915623347

The Strategy Landscape & Core Issues. (n.d.). 1-16. Retrieved January 16, 2018.

Ward, S. (2007). Revisiting African American Leadership. *Pro Quest*. Retrieved October, 2017.

What Is Change Management? (n.d.). Retrieved January 16, 2018, from http://www.prosci.com/change-management/ what-is-change-management

Virtue, M. (2019, February 10). *Employee Champions & Performance Management*. PowerPointPresentation.

Yunus, M. (2009). *Creating a world without poverty: Social business and the future of capitalism*. New York: PublicAffairs.

REFERENCES

12DifferentLeadershipStyles.(n.d.).RetrievedFebruary24,2019,from
    https://wisetoast.com/12-different-types-of-leadership-styles/
Allendar, D. B. (1996). *Leading with a limp.* Colorado Springs,
    Colorado: WaterBrook Press.
Akyeampong, E. (2000). Africans in the Diaspora: The Diaspora and Africa.
    African Affairs, 99(395), 183-215. Retrieved from
    http://ezproxy.eastern.edu:2076/stable/723808
BackMatter.(2012).*The Journal of African American History, 97*(4), 511-
    520.doi:10.5323/jafriamerhist.97.4.bm
Baldwin D. & Makalani M. (Eds.), *Escape from New York: The New
    Negro Renaissance beyond Harlem* (pp. 31-52). University of
    Minnesota Press. Retrieved from http://ezproxy.eastern.
    edu:2076/stable/10.5749/j.ctt4cggkr.5
Bordas,J.(2012).*Salsa, soul, and spirit: leadership for a multicultural age:*.
    Sydney:ReadHowYouWant/Accessible.
Carter, D. (2010). A Nonracial Education: On Navigating Diaspora, Anti-Black
    Caricature, and Anthropology. In *Navigating the African Diaspora:
    The Anthropology of Invisibility* (pp. 35-70). UniversityofMinnesota
    Press. Retrieved from http://ezproxy.
    eastern.edu:2076/stable/10.5749/j.cttttjm0.6
Chude-Sokei, L. (2014). The Newly Black Americans. *Transition,*
    (113), 52-71. doi:10.2979/transition.113.52
Edozie, R., & Gottschalk, K. (2014). Pan-Africanist Globalization and Cultural
    Politics: Promoting the African World View. In *The African Union's
    Africa: New Pan-African Initiatives in Global Governance* (pp. 61-
    96). Michigan State University

Press. Retrieved from http://ezproxy.eastern.edu:2076/stable/10.14321/j.ctt9qf58g.9

JONES, J. (2013). "Brightest Africa" in the New Negro Imagination. In Kelley R. (Author) & Johnson, S. (2016). *Who moved my cheese?* Abbotsford, British Columbia: The Braille Superstore.

Kellerman, B. (2008). *Followership: how followers are creating change and changing leaders.* Boston: Harvard Business Press.

Ng, E. S., & Sears, G. J. (2011). CEO Leadership Styles and the Implementation of Organizational Diversity Practices: Moderating Effects of Social Values and Age. *Journal of Business Ethics, 105*(1), 41-52. doi:10.1007/s10551-011-0933-7

Preskill, S., & Brookfield, S. D. (2009). *Learning as a way of lead- ing: lessons from the struggle for social justice.* San Francisco, CA: Jossey-Bass.

Sen, A. K. (2006). *Identity and violence: the illusion of destiny.* New York: W.W. Norton.

Social Responsibility & Ethics in Marketing. (2018, February 20). Retrieved from https://www.cleverism.com/ social-responsibility-ethics-marketing/

Schamber, A., Dr. (2003). Coaching:Evoking Excellence in God's People. (First Edition), September.

Spears, L. (2005). The Understanding and Practice of Servant-Leadership. *Servant Leadership Research Roundtable,* (August).

Wren, J. T. (1995). *The leader's companion: insights on leadership through the ages.* New York: Free Press.

www.ingramcontent.com/pod-product-compliance
Lightning Source LLC
Chambersburg PA
CBHW052233150726

48002CB00003B/1413